THE
GRIEVE
METHOD

THE
GRIEVE
METHOD

A 7-STEP GUIDE TO HEALING, GROWING, AND REBUILDING LIFE AFTER LOSS

VC
PUBLISHING
2025

BRADLEY VINSON

The GRIEVE Method:

A 7-Step Guide to Healing, Growing, and Rebuilding Life After Loss

For information, contact
VC Publishing
PO Box 536
Argyle, TX 76226
info@vinsoncs.com

ISBN: 979-8-9925783-4-8

Printed in the United States of America

First Edition

To those touched by grief.

TABLE OF CONTENTS

The Role of this Book

Grief is unpredictable. It doesn't come with a map, and it certainly doesn't follow the timelines or expectations of the world around us. Some days, you may feel like you're making progress, only to be knocked down by a wave of sorrow out of nowhere. Other days, you might catch yourself laughing and immediately feel guilty, as if joy is a betrayal of your pain.

This book exists to give you permission.

Permission to grieve in your own way. Permission to take your time. Permission to heal. Permission to hold grief and joy in the same hand. The GRIEVE Method is not about getting over loss—it's about moving through it with intentionality, grace, and the belief that healing is possible.

This book will not give you quick fixes, because there aren't any. But what it will give you is a roadmap. A way to navigate the darkness. A guide to understanding your grief and giving yourself the tools to process it in a way that honors both your loss and your future.

The GRIEVE Method

If you are grieving, I want you to know: you may be bruised or broken, but you are not destroyed. You are not failing. You are becoming—learning to carry your love and loss forward in a way that allows you to live again. This book is your companion on that journey.

Introduction

Grief is a universal experience, but no two people walk through it in the same way, even the mutually shared grief of siblings, spouses, friends, or other relationships. Your grief is uniquely yours. It can feel like an overwhelming, chaotic journey—one that you didn't ask for and certainly weren't prepared to take. This book is designed to be a practical guide, offering tools and insights to help you navigate your grief journey. The GRIEVE Method provides a roadmap, but it's important to understand that there is no specific order or right way to use these tools.

Grief is personal, and you should use what resonates with you in the moment, at your own pace.

While this book focuses on providing practical advice, I believe sharing my personal story is equally important. I'm walking this path and know how isolating it can feel. Throughout the book, I'll interject my experiences—moments of heartbreak, healing, and hope—in call-out boxes. My prayer is that these reflections speak to you at a deeper level, providing comfort and reassurance that you are not alone.

> I remember a time when I felt completely lost in my grief, like I was in a deep fog and couldn't find my way out. But even in that darkness, I clung to my faith. I didn't always have the words to pray, but I knew God was with me, carrying me through those moments when I couldn't carry myself. That faith became my anchor, reminding me that healing was possible, even if I couldn't see it yet.

You need to know that I come to this journey as a Christian, and my belief system and faith have played a significant role in my healing.

My relationship with God has been a constant source of strength, and I've seen how faith can offer hope, even in the darkest moments. If you share this faith, I hope my reflections will provide you with additional support and encouragement. If not, I trust that the practical tools within this book will still offer you guidance and comfort.

No matter where you are on your journey, I hope this book becomes your companion. Whether you need grace, direction, or a sense of peace, The GRIEVE Method is here to help you find your way through. This is not a book about "fixing" grief—it's about learning to live with it, carry it with greater ease, and move toward healing.

G

GRACE FOR THOSE NOT GRIEVING

Grief often feels like a solitary journey.
While deep in our emotions, it's easy to feel isolated from those around us. It can be especially painful when others don't seem to understand or acknowledge the depth of our pain. People may say or do things that feel dismissive or hurtful, whether intentionally or unintentionally. But one of the most powerful tools we can wield during this time is grace—for others and ourselves.

The Struggle to Be Understood
It's natural to expect that those closest to us should intuitively know how to support us through grief. When they fall short, it can create a sense of betrayal or loneliness. Maybe they don't bring up the loss, fearing they'll make us sad. Or perhaps they try to "fix" the pain by offering solutions or platitudes that only deepen our hurt.

1

In these moments, grace becomes essential. Grace is the act of showing kindness, even when others fall short of our expectations. It is not about excusing hurtful behavior but recognizing that everyone navigates grief differently, and many don't know how to help. Offering grace to those who don't understand our pain helps to release the bitterness that can build up when we feel unsupported.

We must remember that the people around us are not grieving our loss and, in most cases, don't even know we're grieving. Some may care deeply, but they haven't felt the earth shift beneath their feet like we have. And truthfully, we wouldn't want them to. The only way they could truly understand would be to experience a loss like ours, and we wouldn't wish that kind of pain on anyone. This is why grace is so important. People often say the wrong things—not because they mean to hurt us but because they're trying to help and don't have the right words.

Most of us, before experiencing deep grief ourselves, have likely done the same. We've offered well-intentioned but unhelpful words, thinking we were bringing comfort. Standing on the other side of that conversation, we see how those words land differently. When we extend grace, we acknowledge that their intent is usually love, even if their execution is flawed. It allows us to release resentment and, when we have the capacity, gently guide them toward a better way to support us.

> Early on in my grief, I was frustrated with everyone, even strangers, who had no idea I was grieving. I would think, "How dare you be shopping, driving on the freeway, and going on with your life when my loved one is dead?!" Maybe I was jealous; I don't know. I think it was partially my desire to have my loved one remembered and cared for by others. I wanted others to see the importance of their life and to grieve them as I was, and it hurt that they didn't.

Giving Grace to Yourself

Grieving is messy. It does not follow a straight line or conform to any timetable. Some days, you may feel like you're handling everything well, while others might feel like you're drowning in sadness. It's easy to be hard on yourself, to expect that you should be "getting over it" or "moving on" by a certain point. But these expectations are unfair and unkind.

Giving yourself grace means acknowledging that grief is a journey that looks different for everyone. It means understanding that you don't have to meet anyone else's expectations—not even your own.

There will be days when you don't have the energy to get out of bed, and that's okay. There will be days when you smile or laugh and then feel guilty about it, and that's okay, too. Grace allows you to feel all of these things without judgment.

Building a Supportive Environment

Offering grace to others can also foster a more supportive environment for your healing. When you show patience and understanding to those who don't understand your grief, you create space for conversations that can bridge the gap between you and your loved ones. Instead of expecting them to know what to say, gently guide them. Let them know how they can support you. Sometimes, people need permission to ask how you're feeling or to sit with you in your sadness without trying to fix anything.

At the same time, know that you are not obligated to be everyone's teacher. If someone continuously dismisses or diminishes your feelings, it's okay to set boundaries. Grace doesn't mean allowing others to hurt you repeatedly; it means prioritizing your well-being while extending kindness where possible.

Practical Steps for Extending Grace

- **Communicate Clearly:** If you have the emotional bandwidth, let those close to you know what kind of support you need. You might say, "I don't need advice right now, but I would appreciate it if you could just listen."

- **Show Compassion to the Unaware:** Not everyone will know you are grieving, and their words or actions may unintentionally sting. Instead of taking offense, try to view these interactions through a lens of grace. Remind yourself that they likely don't mean harm—they simply don't know your story.

- **Give Yourself Permission to Feel:** Allow yourself to experience all the emotions of grief, from sadness and anger to relief and even joy. There is no "right" way to grieve; every feeling is valid.

- **Set Boundaries:** If certain people or situations are too much to handle while grieving, stepping back is okay. Protect your mental and emotional health without guilt.

- **Accept Imperfection:** In yourself and others. No one grieves perfectly. Grace means accepting that you are doing the best you can and that those around you are too, even if they sometimes fall short.

Grace is the foundation that allows healing to take place. It softens the edges of our pain and makes space for the people in our lives to support us—even if they're unsure how to. But most importantly, it allows us to move through grief with empathy for others and self-compassion, knowing that we are doing the best we can in a difficult situation.

Reflective Exercise

Take a moment to reflect on how you've been treating yourself and others during your grief journey. What could you do differently or better?

Write down:

- One way you can show more grace to yourself.
- One way you can extend grace to someone who may not fully understand your grief.

Self-Assessment Questions

- How do I react when others don't respond to my grief the way I expect?
- What expectations do I have of myself during this grieving process? Are they realistic?
- How can I gently communicate my needs to those around me?

R

RELINQUISH CONTROL

Grief often comes with a sense of helplessness. The loss of a loved one disrupts our lives in ways that feel uncontrollable, leaving us searching for ways to regain some sense of order. We try to control our emotions, the reactions of others, or even the timeline for "getting better." But grief doesn't follow rules, and the more we try to control it, the more it can overwhelm us.

We need to realize the power of relinquishing control—allowing ourselves to experience grief without trying to force it into a shape or schedule that doesn't fit. This doesn't mean we're helpless in our healing; instead, it means surrendering to the natural process of grief and trusting that, over time, healing will come.

I believe grief naturally takes us toward healing, but we must participate.

The Illusion of Control

In the early stages of grief, it's common to want to "do something" to feel like we're actively managing the situation. We may find ourselves thinking, If I can keep busy, I won't feel as bad, or If I don't cry, I'll be stronger. But these thoughts are rooted in the false belief that we can control the uncontrollable. Grief, like love, doesn't fit neatly into boxes. It's unpredictable, often showing up at inconvenient times and in unexpected ways.

By trying to control grief, we limit our ability to heal. Repressed or ignored emotions tend to resurface later, often with more intensity. The path to healing requires us to relinquish this illusion of control and instead allow ourselves to feel what we need to feel when we need to.

One of the hardest things to shake is the "what if, should have, could have, why didn't I?" that comes with grief. In grief, pain is a guarantee; suffering is optional and usually self-inflicted. It's the false perception of control that adds so much additional (and unnecessary) suffering and guilt in grief.

Embracing Vulnerability

Letting go of control means embracing vulnerability. This can be difficult, especially if we're used to being the someone others rely on for strength. We might believe that showing our emotions makes us weak or that we must protect others from the depth of our pain. But vulnerability is not a weakness—it's a courageous act of self-acceptance.

Being vulnerable allows us to acknowledge our pain instead of pushing it away. It permits us to cry when we need to, to ask for help when we feel overwhelmed, and to be honest with ourselves and others about where we're really at in our grief journey, even if we don't know.

The Freedom of Letting Go

Relinquishing control brings freedom. When we stop trying to dictate how our grief should unfold, we free ourselves from the pressure to "perform" healing. This doesn't mean we become passive in our healing process, but rather that we approach it with openness and flexibility. Some days will be easier than others, and that's okay. Healing isn't linear, and by letting go, we allow ourselves the grace to move at our own pace.

Letting go can also mean releasing expectations of how others should support us or acknowledge our grief. We may expect our loved ones to say the right things, to know how to comfort us perfectly, or to be available whenever we need them. But just as grief doesn't follow a script, neither do the people around us. Relinquishing control means letting go of these expectations and accepting the support we receive, even if it doesn't look exactly the way we imagined.

Practical Steps for Letting Go

- **Acknowledge the Unpredictability:** Remind yourself that grief will show up when it wants to. Instead of resisting or trying to control it, practice allowing the emotions to come and go naturally. Journal about how you feel in those moments to help process the unpredictability.

- **Ground yourself in the present moment:** Rather than trying to control what comes next, focus on what's happening right now—whether it's tears, frustration, or even moments of peace—without judgment.

- **Set Flexible Expectations:** Allow room for grief when planning your days or weeks. Instead of packing your schedule to avoid your feelings, leave space for rest and reflection. Be gentle with yourself if you can't accomplish everything you planned.

- **Let Go of "Shoulds":** If you catch yourself thinking, "I should be feeling better by now, or I should be stronger," pause and recognize that these are self-imposed expectations. Replace those thoughts with affirmations like, "I'm allowed to feel what I feel, and my healing will take the time it needs."

- **Let Go of Others' Reactions:** You cannot control how others respond to your grief. Release the need for them to understand or say the right things. Instead, focus on your own healing and free others from the burden of carrying your pain.

Finding Peace in Surrender

Surrendering to grief doesn't mean giving up. It means accepting that you can't rush or force healing. By relinquishing control, you give yourself the freedom to experience grief fully, and in doing so, you open the door to deeper healing. As you learn to let go, you'll find that grief becomes less about managing the process and more about finding peace in the journey.

Reflective Exercise

Think of one area where you're trying to control your grief, whether it's your emotions, timeline, or interactions with others. Write about why it feels important to control this aspect and what might happen if you allowed yourself to let go.

Self-Assessment Questions

- What emotions am I trying to control during my grief, and why?

- How can I practice vulnerability with myself and others in this season of life?

- In what ways have I put pressure on myself to "perform" healing or others to care? How can I release that pressure?

I

INVEST IN
YOUR HEALING

Grief, though inevitable, can be an exhausting and consuming journey. Often, we may feel inclined to let it take over without realizing that healing also requires effort—an intentional commitment to prioritize our emotional, mental, and physical well-being. Healing doesn't just happen; we must make deliberate choices to invest in the process to create conditions for recovery.

What does it mean to invest in your healing, not just emotionally but also practically? Healing is a journey, and like any worthwhile endeavor, it demands time, effort, and sometimes even financial resources. By prioritizing yourself this way, you equip yourself to emerge stronger and more whole as you go through grief.

The Importance of "Leaning In"

The idea of leaning into grief may seem counterintuitive—why would we want to focus more on something that hurts so much? But leaning into the pain means acknowledging its presence and engaging with it rather than avoiding or suppressing it. When we lean into our grief, we give ourselves permission to feel deeply and to explore the emotional landscape that comes with loss.

Investing in your healing starts with being present with your grief. It involves committing to self-awareness, accepting that there will be bad days, and being open to whatever emotions arise. Instead of running from those feelings, we allow them to flow, trusting that facing them moves us one step closer to healing.

Prioritizing Self-Care

Investing in your healing also means taking care of your body and mind. Grief can be physically draining, leaving you feeling fatigued, anxious, or even disconnected from your surroundings. In this context, self-care isn't about indulgence; it's about replenishment. It's about ensuring that, despite the pain, you nurture yourself in small but significant ways every day.

Practical self-care steps:

- **Follow the DEER Self-Care Method:** Prioritize your physical needs as a foundational part of healing by remembering D-E-E-R: Drink Water, Eat, Exercise, and Rest. Staying hydrated, nourishing your body, moving gently, and allowing yourself to rest are simple but powerful acts of self-care. By focusing on these basics, you create a solid foundation that supports your emotional and mental well-being through the grief journey.

By paying attention to your basic needs, you build a foundation of strength that can support you as you work through the emotional aspects of healing.

Financial Investment in Healing

Investing in your healing may also mean recognizing when seeking professional help or specialized programming is necessary. This could be through grief counseling, therapy, or even workshops and retreats designed to support individuals in mourning. While there may be a cost associated with these resources, it's crucial to remember that your mental health and emotional recovery are worth the investment.

Consider therapy, conferences, books, etc., not as a last resort but as a proactive step in your healing. These things give you tools, perspective, and a safe space to process your emotions without judgment. The time and resources you spend here invest in your future well-being.

Additionally, these investments tailored to your experience can offer valuable insights and foster a sense of community. These resources can remind you that you're not alone and that healing is possible.

> A word of caution about grief conferences: they can be overwhelming. Though filled with many activities to help you on your healing journey, they can be heavy and very emotional. It's hard to say when the 'right' time on your healing journey to attend one is, but give yourself grace and plan to retreat to your room or private space for a breather occasionally.

Time and Effort: The Priceless Investment

Healing also requires time and effort. While it may be tempting to distract yourself from grief through work, responsibilities, or other commitments, investing in your healing means setting aside time to engage with your emotions actively. This can take many forms: journaling, meditating, talking to trusted friends or family members, or spending quiet moments in reflection.

Invest in Your Healing

The key is to commit to giving grief the attention it demands. This doesn't mean dwelling in sorrow endlessly but dedicating time each day or week to exploring your emotions, practicing self-care, or taking steps toward healing.

Practical Steps for Investing in Your Healing

- **Create a Healing Routine:** Develop daily or weekly rituals prioritizing your emotional and physical health. Whether journaling, attending therapy, or even setting aside time for a relaxing bath, create a routine that allows you to care for yourself in small, meaningful ways.

- **Seek Professional Help:** Consider talking to a grief coach or therapist if you feel stuck or overwhelmed. Therapy is a powerful tool for gaining insight into your grief and learning strategies for managing it.

- **Join a Support Group:** Connecting with others experiencing grief can give you a sense of belonging and understanding. Support groups, whether online or in person, are spaces where you can share your feelings and draw strength from others' experiences.

- **Invest in Personal Development:** Healing isn't just about enduring grief—it's also about growing through it. Invest in resources like books, courses, or workshops that focus on personal growth and resilience during times of loss.

The Long-Term Benefits

While investing in your healing requires time, effort, and sometimes financial resources, it is one of the most important investments you can make. Your healing journey is not passive; it requires active engagement and a willingness to prioritize your well-being. By committing this, you are honoring your loss and emotions and giving yourself the best chance to emerge stronger and more whole.

Healing may not look like you imagined, and it may not happen as quickly as you'd like. But by leaning in, prioritizing self-care, and investing in your journey, you equip yourself with the tools to move forward. Over time, these investments will pay off, helping you not just to survive grief but to thrive despite it.

Reflective Exercise

Consider one way in which you can invest more in your healing. Whether seeking professional help, setting aside more time for self-care, or joining a support group, write down how you can prioritize yourself in this process.

Self-Assessment Questions

- How am I currently taking care of my emotional and physical needs while grieving?

- What resources or support systems can I invest in to help me through this time?

- Am I allowing myself the time and space to heal, or am I pressuring myself to "move on" quickly?

Want to go deeper? Download your free companion workbook!

Healing is not just about reading—it's about applying what you've learned.
The GRIEVE Method Workbook will guide you with reflection prompts, action steps, and exercises to help you heal.

**Get your free workbook now at:
BradleyVinson.com/tgm-workbook**

(Prefer a printed copy? You'll get a special discount after downloading!)

E

EXPRESS YOURSELF & ENGAGE WITH OTHERS

There is power in sharing your grief. Grief is heavy, but it becomes even heavier when carried alone. One of the greatest challenges in grief is the feeling of isolation—the sense that no one truly understands your pain, that your emotions are too much to share, or that people around you are tired of hearing about your loss.

Grief needs an outlet. It needs to be expressed, not buried. Grief wants to be witnessed.

At the same time, healing doesn't happen in isolation. It happens in community. Engaging with others—whether through sharing your story, leaning on friends, or connecting with those who have also experienced loss—allows grief to be witnessed, acknowledged, and processed in a healthy way.

You don't have to grieve alone. You weren't meant to.

Why We Keep Grief to Ourselves

Many people hesitate to express their grief because of fear:

- **Fear of burdening others:** You might think, "People have their own problems. I don't want to bring them down."

- **Fear of judgment:** Worrying that others think you're grieving "too much" or "too long."

- **Fear of vulnerability:** Expressing grief means admitting how deeply we are hurting, which can feel uncomfortable.

- **Fear of losing control:** You may feel that if you start talking about your grief, the emotions will overwhelm you.

These fears are understandable, but they are also obstacles to healing. Grief was never meant to be carried in silence.

Giving Your Grief a Voice

Expressing your grief does not mean standing in front of a crowd and sharing your deepest emotions. It simply means finding an outlet to release what is inside you rather than letting it fester.

Express Yourself & Engage with Others

Different people express grief in different ways. The key is finding the method that feels most natural to you. Here are a few ways you might begin:

- **Talk About Your Loss:** Find a trusted friend, family member, counselor, or support group who will listen without trying to "fix" you. Sometimes, simply saying your thoughts out loud can help you process them.

- **Write It Down:** Journaling can be a powerful way to express grief privately. You can write letters to your loved one, record your emotions, or free-write thoughts. Writing can provide clarity and emotional relief.

- **Express Through Creativity:** Some emotions are too complex for words. Art, music, poetry, dance, and other creative outlets allow grief to take shape in new ways. You don't have to be an artist—just create for the sake of expression.

- **Engage in Physical Expression:** Grief doesn't just exist in your mind—it lives in your body. Movement can help release stored emotions. Walking, exercising, dancing, or even simple breathing exercises can help process the weight of loss.

> I've learned that sweat is an excellent substitute for tears. Taking the time to move has repeatedly helped me escape my slumps during my journey.

- **Allow Yourself to Feel:** Crying, laughing, fear, feeling numb—it's all part of the process. Don't suppress your emotions because you think you "should" be feeling something else. Expression is about honoring whatever emotions are present in the moment.

Expression allows grief to move through you rather than stay stuck inside.

Healing Through Connection

While expressing your grief is important, so is connection. Grief is an isolating experience, but you don't have to go through it alone.

Engaging with others—whether through friendships, support groups, or simple human interaction—reminds you that you are not alone in your pain.

How to Engage With Others While Grieving

- **Lean on a Trusted Support System:** Even if you don't feel like talking, let your close friends or family members be there for you. You don't have to carry the weight alone.

- **Join a Grief Support Group:** Talking to others who have experienced similar losses can be healing. It can also be comforting to know that others genuinely understand what you're going through.

When looking for a group, try several before you pick one. All groups are not made the same. Find a place that supports your journey. Like any other group, grief groups are mostly made of like-minded people. Unfortunately, some grief groups are full of 'stuck' people who are either not ready to heal or have no intention to heal and lean into unhealthy attitudes about the grieving process.

- **Seek Coaching or Therapy:** A professional can provide guidance and a safe space to express your emotions. There's no shame in seeking help—it's a sign of strength.

- **Engage in Acts of Service:** Sometimes, one of the most powerful ways to process grief is by helping others. Volunteering, mentoring, or supporting someone grieving can provide purpose and healing.

- **Find Community in Unexpected Places:** Engaging with others doesn't always mean deep conversations. Sometimes, it's simply being around people—attending a church service, joining a book club, or spending time with a pet. Small interactions can help break the isolation of grief.

Connection doesn't erase grief, but it makes the journey more bearable.

Practical Steps for Expressing & Engaging

- Choose one way to express your grief this week—through talking, art, or movement.

- Reach out to someone—a friend, a support group, or a therapist—and share how you're feeling.

- Engage in a simple social activity—sitting with a friend or attending an event. Small steps matter.

Healing Happens in Community

Grief is deeply personal but not meant to be carried alone. By allowing yourself to express your emotions and engage with others, you create space for healing.

Your grief is real, and your voice matters. There are people who are ready to walk this journey with you right now. You just have to take the first step.

Reflective Exercise

Take a moment to reflect on how you are currently expressing and engaging in your grief journey.

Write down your responses to the following:

- How have I been expressing my grief so far?

- Do I feel like I have been holding anything in? If so, why?

- Who in my life do I feel safe expressing my grief with?

- What is one way I can open myself up to support and connection this week?

Self-Assessment Questions

- Am I allowing myself to express my grief, or am I keeping it bottled up?

- What fears or barriers are preventing me from engaging with others?

- Have I found a healthy outlet for my emotions? If not, what could I try?

- Am I surrounding myself with people who support my healing?

- What small step can I take today to express or engage?

V

VISUALIZE
YOUR HEALING

Grief can often feel like a heavy fog—dense and un-yielding—making it difficult to see beyond the pres-ent moment of pain. Healing may seem distant or even impossible. Yet, one of the most powerful tools for navigating grief is the ability to visualize a future where healing is not only possible but inevitable.

Visualizing healing is not about denying the pain or rushing the process but creating a vision for yourself where peace and joy are once again part of your life. It can provide hope, help you set goals, and make a path forward.

Why Visualization Matters

The mind is a powerful tool. Research has shown that visualizing positive outcomes can influence how we approach challenges, helping shape our emotions and actions. When you are grieving, it can feel like the sadness will never lift. By visualizing your healing, you create a mental map for the future—a future where you have learned to carry your grief with greater ease and where you have made space for joy once again.

Visualization doesn't mean ignoring the pain of grief or pretending it's not there. Instead, it involves acknowledging the pain while believing in the possibility of healing. It allows you to shift your focus, even momentarily, from the heaviness of grief to the hope of recovery. This shift in mindset can provide comfort and remind you that healing, while slow, is possible.

There was a time in my life when sadness felt like it was at the top of a great mountain, high above the valley I was standing in. I just wanted to reach 'sad' and move out of deep, gut-wrenching grief. Eventually, just being sad came, and the following plateau became clearer. This doesn't mean I never slipped on the climb and found myself in a space I thought I had gotten past. Don't let slips diminish your vision of being better.

Imagining a Future Beyond Grief

When you lose someone, it can be hard to imagine life without them. The future you had once envisioned may feel like it no longer exists. But creating a new vision for yourself doesn't mean forgetting your loved one or diminishing your grief. It means envisioning a future where healing is part of your journey.

To begin, take some time to reflect on what healing might look like for you. It may be different for everyone, but consider the following:

- **How would you feel emotionally?** Imagine what it would feel like to experience moments of peace and contentment, even while still honoring your loss.

- **What activities or relationships might bring you joy again?** Picture yourself engaging in activities that once brought you happiness or deepening relationships that provide comfort.

- **How do you want to remember your loved one?**

Visualize ways you can continue to honor their memory in a way that supports your healing rather than keeps you stuck in grief.

This visualization isn't about achieving perfection. It's about allowing yourself to believe that joy can coexist with sorrow and that you can discover a new way of being after loss.

Setting Goals for Healing

Once you've begun to visualize what healing might look like for you, setting small, achievable goals to move toward that vision can be helpful. These goals aren't about forcing yourself to heal quickly but taking intentional steps to support your well-being.

Examples of healing goals might include:

- **Emotional Goals:** "I will allow myself to experience moments of joy without feeling guilty." Or, "I will reach out for support when I need it."

- **Physical Goals:** "I will care for my body by eating nourishing foods and moving regularly." Or "I will create a restful sleep routine to support my mental health."

- **Relational Goals:** "I will seek connection with others, even if it feels difficult, knowing that community is part of my healing." Or, "I will find ways to honor my loved one's memory that feel meaningful to me."

Each goal is a step toward healing. Some days, you may make significant strides; on other days, the goal may be to get through the day. The important thing is to be gentle with yourself and recognize that healing is a gradual process.

Tools for Visualization

There are several ways to engage in visualization as part of your healing process:

- **Guided Imagery:** This technique involves closing your eyes and mentally walking through a peaceful or comforting scene. Imagine yourself in a safe and calm place, and picture your future self feeling lighter, more at peace, or more resilient. You can use guided meditations or recordings to help lead you through this process.

- **Vision Board:** Create a visual representation of what healing looks like for you. Cut out images, words, or symbols from magazines or print them to make a collage. This tangible reminder of your goals can motivate your journey daily.

- **Affirmations:** Write down affirmations that reinforce your belief in healing. "I can heal and find joy again," or "I honor my grief while also creating space for peace." Place these affirmations somewhere you'll see them often, like on your bathroom mirror or refrigerator.

- **Daily Reflection:** Take a few minutes each day to reflect on your progress. Visualize how far you've come, even if the steps seem small. This practice can help reinforce the belief that healing is happening, even on the most challenging days.

- **Set Small Healing Goals:** Write down one or two goals that align with your healing vision. These can be simple, such as "I will take a 10-minute walk each day " or "I will write in my journal about my emotions twice weekly."

Hope for the Future

Grief may feel all-encompassing, but healing is always possible. Visualizing your healing begins to create a new roadmap for your life after loss. This process allows you to see beyond the pain and find hope in the possibility of peace, joy, and resilience. While the journey may be long and the steps small, each moment spent envisioning your future is a step toward making that future a reality.

I used to say, "Always healing, never healed (on this side of eternity)." But I've come to believe something deeper. Healing is possible—but only if we give the Doctor, God, access to our grief. He created our loved ones; He knows the precise shape of the void their absence has left behind. And He can heal it—if we allow Him.

Like any major procedure, healing leaves evidence. There are scars, and there are phantom pains. But being healed doesn't mean forgetting what was broken—it means the wound is no longer open, and the pain no longer controls us. We carry the proof of love and loss but walk forward whole.

Reflective Exercise

Spend 10 minutes visualizing what healing means to you. Picture yourself in a future where you've learned to carry your grief with greater ease. What does this version of yourself look and feel like? Write down your observations and any goals that come to mind.

Self-Assessment Questions

- How do I feel about the possibility of healing? Do I believe it's possible for me?

- What does healing look like for me? How will I know when I've made progress?

- What small goals can I set to help move me closer to the vision I've created for myself?

35

E

ENJOY LIFE

Grief can make joy feel like a betrayal. After a loss, the idea of smiling again, laughing again, or even allowing yourself to dream about the future can feel wrong—like moving forward means leaving your loved one behind. But joy and grief are not opposites. They do not cancel each other out. In fact, they can hold hands.

Think of the person you lost. Would they want you to live in sadness forever? Would they want your life to stop because theirs did? Or would they want you to carry their love forward into a life that is still full, meaningful, and yes—joyful?

You don't have to choose between love and living.

The Guilt of Happiness

One of the biggest struggles after a loss is guilt—especially when moments of happiness come. You might hear a joke and laugh before realizing, as if smiling means you've forgotten your loss. You may experience a moment of peace, only to feel unworthy of it. This guilt is normal, but it's also unnecessary.

Healing doesn't mean forgetting. Joy doesn't mean moving on. Finding happiness again isn't a sign that you love the person you lost any less.

Haven't you always wanted to experience joy and peace in your life? Of course you have. That desire shouldn't change because our loved ones are no longer physically here. You can still honor them and live fully. Finding joy can be one of the most beautiful ways to carry their memory forward.

THIS Life is Still Worth Living

Grief can make life feel empty. After loss, it's common to wonder: What's the point? If the person you loved is no longer here, how can life hold the same meaning?

But grief does not mean the end of your purpose. You still have reasons to be here, things to experience, people to love, and a story to tell. Your life did not end with theirs.

Instead of asking, "What did I lose?" try asking, "What do I still have?"

- You have memories—and the ability to share them.
- You have love—the love you gave and continue to receive.
- You have a future—one that is different but still worth embracing.

Joy does not erase grief. It expands it, allowing healing, hope, and new beginnings.

Practical Steps for Embracing Joy Again

You might not feel ready for joy, and that's perfectly fine. However, healing requires intentional steps, even if they are small. Here are some ideas for reintroducing joy into your life:

- **Find Small Moments of Pleasure:** Joy doesn't have to be big. It can be sipping coffee in the morning, listening to a favorite song, or watching the sunrise. These small moments add up.

- **Allow Laughter:** Laughter is not disrespectful to your grief. It is a release, a reminder that life still holds beauty. Let yourself laugh without guilt.

- **Do Something You Used to Love:** Remember what made you happy before your loss. Maybe it was reading, painting, gardening, or traveling. Start small—engage in that activity, even if just for a few minutes.

- **Create New Traditions:** The old way of life may feel out of reach, and that's okay. You can build new traditions that honor your loved one while allowing you to move forward.
- **Let Go of the Expectation That Joy Must Feel the Same:** Happiness after loss may feel different, but different does not mean bad. It simply means you are growing.

Finding Joy Without Letting Go

The love you have for the person you lost does not disappear just because you are healing. You are not leaving them behind—you are carrying them forward.

Grief and joy are both part of the human experience. One does not cancel out the other. You can miss someone and laugh again, mourn and build new memories.

Your story is not over. Let yourself live.

Reflective Exercise

Take a moment to reflect on the idea of joy after grief. **Grab a journal or a piece of paper and write down your responses to the following:**

- What activities or moments used to bring me joy?

- When was the last time I smiled or laughed? How did it feel?

- What is one small thing I can do this week to experience a moment of happiness?

- If my loved ones were here, how would they encourage me to live fully?

You do not have to force joy, but you can allow it when it comes.

Self-Assessment Questions

- Do I feel guilty when I experience happiness? If so, why?

- Have I allowed myself to embrace small moments of joy, or have I avoided them?

- What is holding me back from believing that I deserve happiness again?

- How can I honor my grief while also making space for joy?

- What is one thing I will do this week to take a step toward enjoying life again?

FREQUENTLY ASKED QUESTIONS (FAQ)

Grief is a deeply personal journey, and while no two experiences are the same, many people who experience loss face common questions and concerns. This FAQ is designed to address some of the most frequently asked questions and provide some guidance.

1. How long does grief last?
There is no set timeline for grief. It's different for everyone and can change over time. Some days may feel more manageable, while others may feel as painful as the first day of loss. It is important to allow yourself the time and space to grieve without rushing the process or expecting it to follow a specific path. Grief may never fully disappear, but over time, you'll learn to live with it and find ways to experience moments of peace and joy again.

2. Is it normal to feel okay sometimes and then feel sad again?

Yes, it's completely normal. Grief is not linear. You may have days or moments when you feel "normal" or even happy and then suddenly be overwhelmed by sadness again. This is part of the natural 'ebb and flow' of grief. Allow yourself to feel whatever emotions come up without judgment.

3. How can I support myself when others don't understand my grief?

It can be difficult when those around you don't understand your grief or don't know how to support you. It's important to communicate your needs clearly. Let your loved ones know how they can help by simply listening, offering companionship, or giving you space. If you feel unsupported, consider seeking out a support group or professional help that can provide the compassion you need.

4. How do I handle the guilt I feel when I experience joy after a loss?

Feeling joy or happiness after a loss doesn't mean you've forgotten your loved one or are "moving on" without them. Joy and grief can hold hands. It's essential to permit yourself to feel happy when those moments come. Honor your grief, but allow yourself to embrace moments of joy without guilt.

5. I'm afraid that if I express my emotions, they will overwhelm me. What can I do?

It's common to fear that expressing your emotions will be overwhelming, but bottling them up can lead to more pain in the long run. Start small. Whether you talk to someone you trust, write in a journal, or engage in creative expression like drawing or painting, releasing your emotions in manageable ways can help you process your grief in a healthy way. If the emotions feel too intense, seeking help from a therapist can provide you with guidance and tools to manage them safely.

6. How can I help my children or other family members who are also grieving?

Children and family members grieve in different ways. Creating an open, honest space where they feel comfortable expressing their emotions is important. Be patient, listen to their concerns, and tell them it's okay to feel sad, angry, or confused.

7. Will I ever feel normal again?

After a loss, your sense of "normal" may shift. You will likely develop a new way of being that incorporates both the memory of your loved one and the healing that comes with time. While things may not return to how they were before the loss, you can still find peace, joy, and purpose as you heal.

8. What are some ways to honor the memory of my loved one?

There are many meaningful ways to honor the memory of a loved one. You can create new traditions, such as lighting a candle on important dates, starting a memorial fund in their name, or dedicating a personal project or act of kindness to them. The most important thing is to find a way that feels right for you—something that brings comfort and meaning to your healing journey.

9. I don't want to make people sad or bring them down with my tears. How do I handle this?

I lean on my 100/0 Rule to help with this: You are 100% in control of sharing your grief with others, but you are 0% in control of how they respond. Your only responsibility is to express your grief honestly—how others react is up to them, not you. Free yourself from the burden of managing their emotions and focus on what you need to heal.

EMBRACING HEALING

Grief is a journey no one chooses, yet it's one that we all face at some point in life. It changes us, leaving us forever marked by the loss of someone we loved. But while grief may alter our path, it doesn't have to define our entire future. Healing is possible, and it begins with grace and an intentional choice to move forward, even when the way is unclear.

Throughout this book, we've explored The GRIEVE Method, a roadmap designed to help you navigate the complex terrain of grief. Each step, from showing grace to yourself and others to relinquishing control to visualizing healing, is a small piece of the puzzle that leads to a life beyond the pain of loss. This process doesn't happen overnight, and it isn't a linear path. Grief ebbs and flows, and so does healing.

Healing as a Continuous Process

Healing doesn't mean forgetting your loss or no longer feeling its pain. It means learning to carry that pain in a way that doesn't prevent you from living a meaningful, joyful life. It means finding ways to honor your loved one while creating space for new experiences, relationships, and happiness.

There will be days when you feel like you've made progress and other days when the grief feels as fresh as the day it began. This is normal. The journey of healing is not about "getting over" your grief but about learning how to live with it in a way that allows you to find peace, joy, and purpose once again.

Embracing the New You

The person you were before your loss is not the same person you are now. Grief changes us—sometimes in ways we don't expect. However, with time, we can learn to embrace the "new you" that emerges after loss. This doesn't mean you're leaving your loved one behind or moving on without them. Instead, it means you're integrating their memory into your life in a way that allows you to keep moving forward.

Embracing this new normal may involve finding new traditions, engaging in activities that bring you peace, or deepening relationships with those around you. It also means allowing yourself to dream again, setting new goals, and envisioning a future where joy and grief can coexist.

Honoring the Memory of Your Loved One

Part of healing is finding meaningful and healing ways to honor your loved one's memory. This could involve creating traditions, such as lighting a candle on significant dates or celebrating their life through charitable acts or creative expression. However you honor them, know that this process is personal and unique to you.

By keeping their memory alive in ways that bring you peace, you carry them with you on your journey forward. Grief and healing are intertwined; acknowledging both creates a space where healing can flourish.

A Journey Shared

While grief can feel isolating, remember that you are not alone in this journey. Countless others have walked this path, and many continue to walk it with you now. Whether through friends, family, or faith communities, shared experiences can provide strength. Healing is as much a collective journey as it is a personal one, and finding people to walk alongside you can make all the difference.

As you move forward, continue to connect with those around you who understand and support your healing journey. Let them uplift you when you feel weak and celebrate your progress, no matter how small. Healing is not something you have to face alone.

Applying The GRIEVE Method

The GRIEVE Method is more than just a set of principles—it's a practice. Grief is unpredictable, so consider it a toolbox rather than seeing this method as a checklist. Some days, you may need to extend grace to yourself when you feel like you're "not doing enough." Other days, you may need to relinquish control when grief feels chaotic.

Each element of The GRIEVE Method offers practical ways to process your grief and move forward, step by step. Here's how you can apply it to your life:

- **Grace for Those Not Grieving**: Acknowledge that some people may not understand your grief. Let go of unrealistic expectations—of both others and yourself.

- **Relinquish Control:** Let go of the idea that grief follows a set timeline. Allow your emotions to flow without judgment.

- **Invest in Your Healing:** Look for support, whether through therapy, journaling, creative expression, or self-care.

Embracing Healing

- **Express & Engage:** Find ways to express your grief (talking, writing, art, movement) and engage with supportive people. Healing happens in community.

- **Visualize Your Healing:** Picture what healing looks like for you. Set small, manageable goals that help you move forward and reach them.

- **Enjoy Life:** Give yourself permission to experience happiness again, knowing that joy and grief can hold hands.

Grief is not a linear process. You may cycle through these steps repeatedly, and that's okay. Healing is not about "moving on"—it's about carrying your grief in a way that allows you to keep living.

A Final Word

Grief is something you carry with you, and that's okay. Over time, its weight will shift. You will grow stronger and find ways to live with your loss(es). This journey is difficult, but it can lead to profound growth, deepened compassion, and a renewed sense of purpose.

I pray you carry forward the tools and insights shared in these pages. I hope they comfort you and guide you toward a healing, loving, and peace-filled future. Remember, you are not alone; healing is possible—even in the darkest moments.

May you find strength in your journey, hope in your healing, and love in every step you take forward.

ADDITIONAL RESOURCES

Grief is a challenging journey; having the right resources can help you heal. Whether you seek books, support groups, counseling, or online communities, countless tools are available to help you navigate grief. However, as new resources are continually being developed, I believe it's important to keep this information as current and comprehensive as possible.

For that reason, rather than listing all available resources here, I've created a comprehensive and regularly updated list on my website. This allows me to keep the information fresh and relevant, ensuring that you have access to the latest and most helpful tools as they become available.

By visiting my website, you can find:
- Recommended books on grief and healing.
- Support groups for different types of loss.
- Online resources and forums for connecting with others on a similar journey.
- Workshops, conferences, and retreats focused on emotional healing and recovery.

I invite you to visit my website for this growing list of grief-related resources. Whether you are looking for personal support, professional guidance, or a sense of community, you will find resources to help you along the way.

**To view the complete and updated list
of grief resources,
please visit BradleyVinson.com/resources**

This page will continue to be updated as I discover new tools, support networks, and books to aid you further in your healing journey. Please check back regularly for the most up-to-date information, and feel free to pass on the link to others.

YOUR NEXT STEPS

Congratulations Congratulations on completing **The GRIEVE Method: A 7-Step Guide to Healing, Growing, and Rebuilding Life After Loss.** Healing is a journey; you don't have to walk it alone. Here are a few ways to continue your growth and find additional support:

1. **Download Your Free GRIEVE Method Workbook:** Sometimes, applying everything you're learning is hard. This free workbook will guide you through each step of The GRIEVE Method, helping you process your emotions and take action toward healing. BradleyVinson.com/tgm-workbook

2. **Book Bradley for a Workshop or Speaking Event:** Do you lead a church, grief group, or caregiver organization? Bring this content to your community as an engaging workshop, training, or keynote presentation. BradleyVinson.com/speaking

3. Bulk Orders for Groups, Churches, & Caregivers:
Equip your community with a practical guide
to grief. Special discounts are available for bulk
orders of 10+ books.

For bulk purchase inquiries, email:
info@bradleyvinson.com with the subject line
"Bulk Order Inquiry."

4. Get Personal Support (1:1 Coaching): If you
want personalized guidance on your healing
journey, explore 1:1 grief coaching and
structured support options. Learn more at
BradleyVinson.com/coaching

You don't have to walk this journey alone. Healing is
possible, and I'm here to support you every step of
the way.

Visit BradleyVinson.com to continue your journey.

The GRIEVE Method®

GRACE for those not grieving

RELINQUISH control

ENJOY life

INVEST in your healing

VISUALIZE a better future

EXPRESS yourself & **E**NGAGE with others

COMPASSION

ACCEPTANCE

TRANSFORMATION

INSPIRATION

CONNECTION

EMPOWERMENT

www.ingramcontent.com/pod-product-compliance
Lightning Source LLC
Chambersburg PA
CBHW052218090426
42741CB00010B/2593